T-Shirt Yarn

PROJECTS TO CROCHET AND KNIT

Sandra Lebrun

STACKPOLE BOOKS

The publisher would like to thank DMC, who provided the materials used in this book.
Hoooked products are distributed exclusively by DMC in France, Spain, Italy,
the United Kingdom, and Japan.

Go to www.dmc.com to find the retailer nearest to you.

The author would like to thank the passionate women, both novices and experts, at the
creative workshop "Des fils en aiguilles," of Paizay-Naudouin in Charente, for their wise advice.

Originally published as *Tricoter et Crocheter avec le fil coton XXL* by Dessain et
Tolra/Editions Larousse

Original French edition © Dessain et Tolra 2013

English language edition © Stackpole Books 2014
Published by
STACKPOLE BOOKS
5067 Ritter Road
Mechanicsburg, PA 17055
www.stackpolebooks.com

Printed in the United States of America
10 9 8 7 6 5 4 3 2 1
First edition

Editorial direction: Colette Hanicotte
Editorial and artistic coordination:
    Corinne de Montalembert
Interior design: Anoï
Photography and styling: Cactus Studio
Technique photos: Olivier Ploton
Illustrations: Sandra Lebrun
Cover design: Tessa J. Sweigert
Translation: Kathryn Fulton

Read and approved by Ploom

Library of Congress Cataloging-in-Publication Data

Lebrun, Sandra.
    [Tricoter et crocheter avec le fil coton XXL. English]
    T-shirt yarn : projects to crochet and knit / Sandra Lebrun. — First edition.
        pages cm
    Translation of: Tricoter et crocheter avec le fil coton XXL.
    ISBN 978-0-8117-1453-2
    1. Crocheting—Patterns.   2. Knitting—Patterns.   3. Textile waste—Recycling.
4. T-shirts.   I. Title.
    TT825.L3882613 2014
    746.43'4—dc23
                                    2014014767

Contents

Introduction

Accessories

Home Décor

ⵝ Knitted project
| Crocheted project
The number of asterisks after each project name indicates the level of difficulty.

The craft and the materials

A rich and varied fiber

There's no need to be an expert to knit or crochet with recycled T-shirt yarn. It's the ideal material for beginners! And if you are already familiar with one of these crafts, the fiber will make the experience new and exciting. With T-shirt yarn, the work goes much faster, and your hand movements will adapt to this fun material. The variation between yarns from one ball to another will pleasantly surprise you as you work.

With hook or needles in hand, brush up on your skills on the next few pages—or jump right in to your T-shirt yarn project.

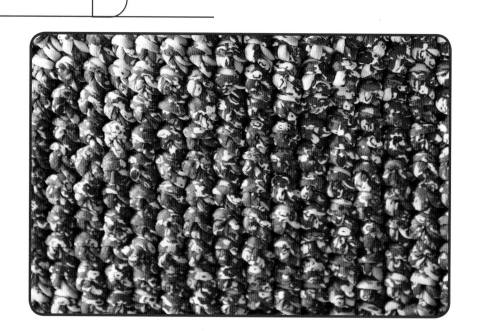

The adventure of recycled fiber

The idea of recycling—and, in general, of reducing waste—is prominent in our thoughts today. T-shirt yarn is, as the name implies, made from excess fabric left over from factories that make T-shirts and other knit fabrics. These leftovers, usually discarded, are recovered and repurposed to make a great fiber to knit and crochet with.

In this way, this trendy fiber sliding between your fingers, with its colorful motifs that give it so much of it's richness, will have—thanks to your creations—a second life.

And the adventures continue . . .

Sandra Lebrun

Things to know

This is a book for beginning knitters and crocheters and only uses the basic stitches; you don't need any special skills to make any of these projects. [And to make the patterns easier to read for beginners, I do not use any abbreviations in the instructions.]

T-shirt yarn comes from recycled fabric and is often available only in whatever colors or patterns were on hand at a particular time. Always make sure you have enough of the color you're using to make the whole project; you may not be able to purchase more of the same color or pattern later on.

The instructions for the projects are not always exact. Often, they are written to be adapted to the material you are using and the use you have in mind for the project. T-shirt yarn is a flexible material to work with and allows you to relax and let your creativity flow.

The elasticity and thickness of this fiber allows you to make most projects with it very quickly. It also allows you to knit and reknit fabric over and over without the yarn unraveling. Crocheters and knitters know that reknitting is often something we have to do a lot!

Since different T-shirt yarns may be very different in thickness or other factors, it's best to make these projects based on actual size rather than the number of stitches.

Choose your crochet hook or knitting needles according to the thickness of your yarn. For simplicity, all the projects in this book were made with 12 mm hooks and needles; you may substitute any close size (such as a size P-15 crochet hook or size 15 knitting needles, both 10 mm) that gives you a finished fabric you're happy with.

Ready? Then onward to the stitches!

Knitting: basic techniques

Casting on

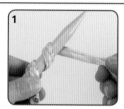

Wrap the yarn twice around the needle.

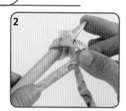

Pick up the first loop and pull it up and over the second one.

Place the loop you just picked up behind the point of the needle.

Wrap the yarn around the needle two more times.

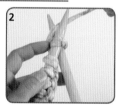

Pass the first of the two new loops over the second. Continue to repeat steps 4 and 5 until you have the number of stitches you need on the needle.

Use your left thumb to hold down the beginning yarn end. You can let go of it once you have cast on the second stitch.

Knit stitch

Insert the right-hand needle (for right-handed knitters; left-handed knitters will work in mirror image of these instructions) under the first stitch from bottom to top.

Bring the yarn around behind and then between the two needles.

Hold the yarn down along the right-hand needle.

Without losing the yarn, bring the right-hand needle back through the stitch to the front.

Bring the stitch you just worked through to the top of the left-hand needle and slip it off.

The first stitch has been worked and passed from the left-hand needle to the right-hand needle.

Purl stitch

With the yarn in front of the work, insert the right-hand needle into the stitch from top to bottom.

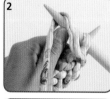

Bring the yarn around the right-hand needle.

Bring the right-hand needle back through the stitch, bringing the yarn with it.

Bring the stitch you just worked through to the top of your left-hand needle and slip it off.

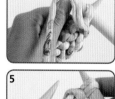

The purl stitch is complete.

When working purl stitches, the yarn must be to the front of the work.

Binding off

1 To finish off a piece of knitting, work the first two stitches. Pick up the first stitch.

2 Pass that stitch over the second stitch.

3 Place the stitch under the needle. Knit another stitch and repeat, passing the old stitch over the new one. Continue in this manner until one stitch remains.

Fastening off

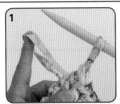

1 All the stitches have been bound off and only one loop is left.

2 Cut the working yarn, leaving as long a tail as you need (see tip below).

3 Pull the remaining loop to open it up a bit, then pass the cut end of the yarn through it.

4 Pull on the cut end of the yarn to tighten the loop securely.

The tail left over after fastening off the work will usually be woven into the fabric to hide it. Sometimes, you will use the tail to assemble a piece; in this case, you will need to leave a longer tail.

Weaving in ends

1 Use a yarn needle to weave the end of the yarn into the stitches of the knitted fabric on the wrong side.

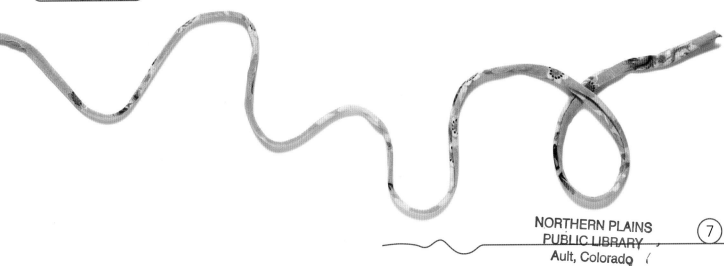

Crochet: basic techniques

Holding the hook

1 Hold the crochet hook in your dominant hand. There are two ways to hold it: You can hold it like a pencil, with your hand underneath.

2 Or you can hold the hook with your hand above it.

It doesn't matter which way you hold the hook; just use the position that feels most natural to you.

The starting knot

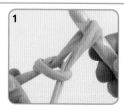

1 Make a loop from the yarn, then catch the end of the yarn connected to the ball (the working yarn) and pull it through the loop.

2 Pull to tighten the knot and adjust it snugly around the crochet hook.

The starting knot is also called a "slip knot."

Chain stitch

1 Starting with the yarn behind the hook, bring the yarn around the hook to the front; this is called a "yarn over."

2 Hold onto the base of the starting knot and use the tip of the hook to catch the yarn over.

3 Pull the yarn through the loop with the crochet hook.

4 A new loop is on the hook and a chain stitch has been made. Yarn over and pull the yarn through the new loop to make another chain. Continue until you have the number of chains called for in the instructions.

The chain stitch is the base for all crochet projects. When you finish the starting chain, you will begin working from right to left.

Slip stitch

 **1** Locate the stitch where you want to make the slip stitch. (Here, we will make the stitch in the second chain stitch from the hook, right above the thumb in the photo.)

 **2** Insert the hook through the stitch.

 **3** Yarn over.

 **4** Use the crochet hook to pull the yarn through the stitch you are working in.

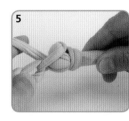 **5** When you get the yarn through the stitch, keep going to go through the loop on the hook as well.

 **6** Pull the yarn through the loop.

 **7** Slip stitch completed.

 Pull on the yarn to adjust the loop on the hook after completing a stitch.

Single crochet

 **1** Locate the stitch where you want to make the single crochet. (Again, we will work into the second chain stitch from the hook, right above the thumb in the photo.)

 **2** Insert the hook into the stitch.

 **3** Yarn over.

 **4** Pull the yarn through the stitch and stop there.

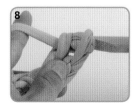 **5** There are 2 loops on the hook.

 **6** Yarn over again.

 **7** Pull the yarn through both loops on the hook.

8 Once you pull the yarn through, you will have 1 loop on the hook and 1 single crochet stitch completed.

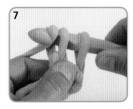 After completing the stitch, pull on the yarn to adjust the loop on the hook.

More crochet techniques

Increasing

Work up to the stitch where you want to add a stitch, then work a stitch (slip stitch or single crochet, depending on the pattern) in that stitch as normal.

Work another stitch in the same space, inserting the hook into the same stitch as you did in step 1.

Decreasing

To reduce the number of stitches, simply skip one. Here, the hook is pointing to the next stitch. Do not insert the hook into this stitch.

Insert the hook into the next stitch and work it as normal.

Turning

When you get to the end of a row, you need to turn the work.

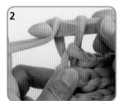

Before you turn, work 1 chain stitch.

The chain stitch will be the starting point for the next row of crocheting. Turn the piece like the page of a book and start working again from right to left.

Crocheting in the round

Chain 5.

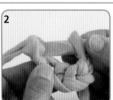

Insert the hook into the first chain.

Yarn over.

Pull the yarn through the chain and through the loop on the hook (slip stitch formed).

The work is joined in the round and ready for you to keep working from right to left.

When you work in the round, you will need to increase, adding stitches in each round, if you want the work to lie flat.

Counting stitches

This chain is composed of 6 stitches. The knot at the end does not count as a stitch.

The loop on the crochet hook does not count as a stitch.

The stitches are counted in the same way in the beginning chain and in later rows.

Different ways of working into a stitch

You can work in the front loop of a stitch by inserting the hook under only the front strand of the stitch.

You can also work into the back loop of a stitch in the same way.

You can also work through both loops by inserting the hook under both strands of yarn at once. Unless the pattern instructs otherwise, this is how you should work into all stitches.

Fastening off

When you finish crocheting a piece, cut the yarn.

Pull on the loop to pull the cut end of yarn out of the last stitch and tighten the stitch around the yarn.

Use a yarn needle to weave the cut end of yarn into the fabric to hide it.

Assembling pieces

There are a few ways to assemble two pieces of crocheted fabric. You can crochet them together with slip stitch.

Or with single crochet.

You can also use a yarn needle to sew the two pieces together.

14

22

30

Accessories

38

White scarf

A scarf is the perfect first knitting project. This one uses both knit and purl stitches, but you could make the whole thing with knit stitches, if you prefer.

- a pair of 12 mm straight knitting needles
- 1 ball of white T-shirt yarn
- scissors
- yarn needle
- assorted beads
- sewing needle
- white sewing thread

Cast on 12 stitches (see page 6) onto one needle.

Tie a piece of scrap yarn around the other needle for reference.

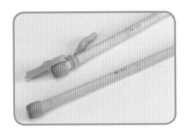

Knit all the stitches on the first row. Knit the second and third rows as well.

Purl the fourth row. (You will be working with the marked needle on this row.)

Repeat step 3, knitting the next 3 rows.

Repeat step 4, purling the next row.

Continue to repeat this pattern of 4 rows until the scarf is the desired length.

Bind off the stitches, fasten off the work, and use a yarn needle to weave in the ends at the beginning and end of the piece.

Using the sewing needle and thread, sew beads at each end of the scarf as desired.

 Tip:

Choose a recycled yarn that isn't too stretchy for this project, so that your scarf doesn't stretch out of shape.

 Skills:

For how to cast on, knit, purl, and bind off stitches, see the techniques on pages 6 and 7.

Yarn and needles:

Don't hesitate to use larger or smaller needles, as needed to match your yarn.

Black headband

This ear warmer is the perfect thing to keep you warm in winter. Customize it to fit exactly. Mixing up knit and purl rows gives this headband a simple texture pattern.

- a pair of 12 mm straight knitting needles
- 1 ball of black T-shirt yarn
- scissors
- yarn needle

 Cast on 8 stitches onto one needle.

 Tie a piece of scrap yarn around the other needle for reference.

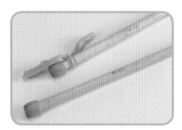

 Knit all the stitches on the first row. The 8 stitches will be passed from the first needle to the marked needle.

 On the next row, purl all the stitches. Every time you purl a row, check that the stitches to be worked are on the marked needle.

 Repeat the last two steps for rows 3 and 4: 1 row of knit stitches and 1 row of purl stitches.

 Knit the next 4 rows (rows 5–8).

 Start over again at the beginning of the 8-row pattern; alternate knit and purl for 4 rows, then knit for 4 rows.

 Stop knitting when your headband is long enough to go around your head, and bind off the stitches.

 Fasten off the work, leaving a long tail. Use the tail and a yarn needle to sew the ends of the headband together, sewing the seam with the right sides of the fabric together. Use a yarn needle to weave the yarn ends into the fabric.

Variation:

If you prefer a headband without the raised ridges, alternate rows of knit and purl the whole way around (i.e., omit step 6).

Tip:

For a good fit, choose a very stretchy yarn.

Using up scraps:

This headband doesn't require very much yarn, so it's a good project for using up small amounts of leftover yarn.

Small blue purse

A cell phone, a pair of glasses, and a packet of tissues will fit in this casual little purse.

- 12 mm crochet hook
- 1 ball of blue T-shirt yarn
- tape measure
- scissors
- 1 button
- sewing thread
- sewing needle
- yarn needle

1
Start with a slip knot, then chain 15.

2
Starting in the second chain from the hook, slip stitch in each chain across, working in the back loop only.

3
When you get to the end of the chain, work 3 slip stitches in the last chain.

4
Slip stitch around the other side of the chain, working in the unworked loop of each chain; work 3 slip stitches in the last chain to turn the corner.

5
Continue to work a slip stitch in each stitch, working in a continuous spiral around the piece, until your purse is about 10 in. (25 cm) tall. The piece will be shaped like a flat, square pocket.

6
Make the flap of the purse by working across only the first half of the stitches. Stop and make 1 chain stitch.

7
Turn the piece around and work back across the stitches for the flap. When you get to the end, work 1 chain stitch and then turn. Continue working back and forth until the flap measures 4 in. (10 cm). Fasten off the work.

8
Join the yarn at one of the top corners of the purse by placing a slip knot on the hook and then working a slip stitch through the fabric of the purse where you want to join the yarn. Chain 60. Slip stitch in the opposite corner of the purse to attach the strap there.

9
Work slip stitches back along the strap until you reach the end where you started. Slip stitch in the purse, then work slip stitches back along the back edge of the chain. Finish with a final slip stitch in the opposite corner of the purse, then fasten off. Use a yarn needle to weave the yarn ends into the fabric.

 The shape:
After steps 3 and 4, your work will be flat. Continue to crochet as described in step 5 and the purse shape will emerge.

 The button:
Make a loop of yarn and tie it to the flap with the knot on the inside. Sew the button to the front of the bag in the corresponding position.

 The strap:
If your yarn is thin, don't hesitate to work a fourth or fifth row of slip stitch along the strap.

Ballerina slippers

This pair of slippers is made entirely with single crochet stitches worked in the back loops.

- 12 mm crochet hook
- 1 ball of fine blue T-shirt yarn
- 1 ball of fine white T-shirt yarn
- scissors
- tape measure
- yarn needle

 Start by making a chain of 11 stitches with the blue yarn.

 Single crochet in the second chain from the hook and in each chain across, working through the back loops. Chain 1, then turn the work.

 Work another row of single crochet through the back loops; chain 1, then turn.

 In the next row of single crochet, increase 2 stitches: Work 2 stitches in the first stitch, then crochet across the row to the last stitch, and work 2 stitches in the last stitch. Continue to work rows of straight single crochet (no increasing or decreasing) until the work is as long as the distance between your heel and the widest part of your foot.

 Decrease 2 stitches in the next row by skipping the second stitch at the beginning and the second-to-last stitch. Do the same in the following 3 rows (4 decrease rows in all, 8 stitches decreased).

 Work the next 3 rows even, without increasing or decreasing. The work should be bottle-shaped.

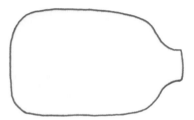

 Fold the edges of the piece up as shown below, and sew the back of the heel. Fold up the point of the slipper and sew the edges together.

 Add a row of single crochet with white yarn all the way around the opening of the slipper. Join the end of the edging row to the first stitch with a slip stitch and fasten off. Use a yarn needle to thread a length of white yarn through this top row; tie this yarn off at the front of the slipper in a bow. Use a yarn needle to weave any other yarn ends into the fabric.

 Size:
A starting chain of 11 stitches will yield a women's size 7–8 slipper. For a larger or smaller slipper, make the starting chain longer or shorter, respectively, and check the fit often as you crochet.

 The ties:
The tie that goes around the top edge of the slipper should pass under the strands of white yarn that make the joint between the two colors.

 Adjust:
Try the slipper on frequently as you make it and adjust the fit by increasing or decreasing stitches if needed.

Red handbag

This round bag, which closes with a drawstring like a coin purse, is easier to make than it appears. Its flexible shape adjusts to its contents.

- 12 mm crochet hook
- 1 ball of dark red T-shirt yarn
- 2 round plastic or wood purse handles
- tape measure
- scissors
- yarn needle
- 4 large wooden beads

Start with a ring: Chain 5, then work a slip stitch in the first chain to join the piece into a ring.

Single crochet around the ring, working in the back loop only of each chain stitch. When you get to the beginning, continue to work in a continuous spiral around the piece, increasing 1 stitch every 3 stitches to keep a flat circle shape.

Continue single crocheting around the piece, increasing evenly, until you have a flat circle 8 in. (20 cm) in diameter.

Work 3 rounds even in single crochet, without increasing or decreasing.

Continue to single crochet around the piece, decreasing 1 stitch each round (by skipping a stitch), varying the placement of the skipped stitch so that the piece gets smaller evenly.

Stop decreasing when the bag is about 8 in. (20 cm) tall.

Attach the handles by crocheting through them: On each stitch along the top edge where the handle should lie, insert the hook into the stitch, then yarn over once in front of the handle and once behind the handle, then complete the stitch as normal. Fasten off and use a yarn needle to weave the yarn ends into the fabric. Alternatively, if this is easier for you, you can simply sew the handles to the purse with the yarn needle and the same yarn you used to make the bag.

Use the yarn needle to thread two lengths of yarn through the stitches around the top edge of the bag, letting the ends hang out on either side of the bag. Thread a bead onto the end of each strand of yarn and tie off the end to hold the bead in place.

 Increasing:

Adjust the increases to match your yarn. If the bottom of the bag is not flat enough, increase every 2 stitches instead of every 3. If the bottom piece warps, increase every 4 stitches.

 Tip:

When working in the round, it can be easy to lose track of the beginning of the round. You can make it easier on yourself by marking the first stitch of the round with a small piece of scrap yarn in a contrasting color.

Variation:

The purse shown here has two handles, but you could replace them with a small strap (such as the one used on the bag on page 18).

Blue beanie

This beanie is crocheted from the brim up, using decreases for the shaping. If you prefer increases, adapt the pattern for the pink hat (see page 30), which is worked from the top down.

- 12 mm crochet hook
- 1 ball of blue T-shirt yarn
- tape measure
- scissors
- yarn needle

1 Start by working a chain long enough to go around your head.

2 Work a slip stitch in the first chain to join the chain into a circle.

3 Work two rounds of single crochet around the circle, working through the back loop only of each stitch.

4 On the third and fourth rounds of the hat, decrease by skipping every 10th stitch.

5 Work the fifth round even in single crochet, without increasing or decreasing.

6 Work another two decrease rounds, skipping every 10th stitch.

7 In the next two rounds, skip every 6th stitch. Next work a round where you decrease every 3rd stitch; finally, work a round where you skip every other stitch.

8 Close up the top of the hat by working 3 single crochets evenly spaced around the opening.

9 Turn the hat inside out. Work a border of two rows of single crochet around the bottom edge of the hat. Join the end of the last row by working a slip stitch in the first stitch of the row, then fasten off. Use the yarn needle to weave the yarn ends into the fabric.

 Tip:
It can be difficult to remember where the beginning of the round is when working in the round. You can mark it for yourself by threading a small scrap of yarn in a different color through the first stitch of each round.

 Customizing the hat:
Try the beanie on often as you make it; this will allow you to adapt the instructions to the size needed and the stretchiness of your yarn.

 The bow:
To make the little bow, wrap the yarn 4 times around your fingers and tie the wraps off around the middle with another small piece of yarn.

Mottled tube purse

Making this tube-shaped purse requires a little bit of organization. Take the time to measure the best length to correspond to your strap, to test the placement of the buttons, and to make sure all three button loops are the same length. You'll be glad you put in the extra effort!

- 12 mm crochet hook
- 1 ball of mottled T-shirt yarn
- tape measure
- scissors
- yarn needle
- 3 buttons
- 1 premade purse strap

 Start by making a ring: Chain 5, then work a slip stitch in the first chain to join it into a ring.

 Single crochet around the ring, working through the back loop only of each stitch. Increase 1 stitch (by working 2 stitches in a single space; see page 10) every other stitch.

 Continue around the circle, increasing every 2 stitches, until the piece measures 5 in. (13 cm) in diameter. Fasten off, leaving a long tail to use when assembling the purse.

 Repeat steps 1–3 to make another circle the same size as the first.

 Begin the main rectangle for the purse by making a chain about 12 in. (30 cm) long, or your desired length (try out your strap to figure out the best width for the purse).

 Chain 1, then slip stitch along the length of the chain, starting in the second chain from the hook and working through the back loop only of each stitch. As always, chain 1 before turning the work.

 Continue to work back and forth in slip stitches through the back loops until the piece is long enough to go around the edge of the end circles. Work 3 more rows for the flap.

 Lay out the rectangle and place a circle at each end. Attach the edge of one circle to the edge of the rectangle by working slip stitches through both layers of fabric. Go all the way around the edge of the circle, but do not close the opening off entirely. Fasten off, then attach the other circle in the same way, starting and stopping in the same places as for the first circle. Fasten off.

 Use the yarn needle to sew the strap to the purse. Make three loops of yarn and tie them to the flap with the knots on the inside. Sew the buttons to the front of the purse just under the loops.

 Construction:
This purse is composed of two circles for the ends and a rectangle that wraps around them to form the body of the bag and the flap.

 Tip:
Choose a very thick, stretchy yarn for the project to give the bag a good sturdiness.

 The circles:
If a circle warps, increase less often. If a circle curves like a cup, increase more often.

Blue cowl

This seed stitch cowl makes a warm and elegant neck warmer.

- a pair of 12 mm straight knitting needles
- 2 balls of blue T-shirt yarn
- scissors
- yarn needle
- tape measure

 Cast on 31 stitches onto one knitting needle.

 Knit the first stitch. Bring the yarn to the front of the work and purl the second stitch.

 Bring the yarn back to the back of the work and knit the next stitch; then bring it to the front of the work and purl the next stitch. Continue in this pattern, alternating between 1 knit stitch and 1 purl stitch, to the end of the row. Because you started with a knit stitch, your last stitch should also be a knit stitch.

 Turn the work and work the second row the same as the first, beginning with 1 knit stitch and alternating between knit and purl.

 Continue to work back and forth in rows, starting each row with a knit stitch, until the piece is about 40 in. (1 m) long.

 Bind off all the stitches and fasten off the work. You should have a rectangle of fabric at this point.

 Put a half twist in the rectangle by laying it out flat and then turning one end over. Without adding or losing any twists, bring one end to the other and sew the ends of the piece together using a yarn needle. This mobius shape will give the cowl an elegant and flexible look. Use the yarn needle to weave in any yarn ends.

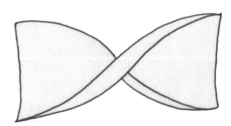

 Tip:
Working in seed stitch is easiest if you work over an odd number of stitches. This way you will always start and end each row with the same kind of stitch.

 Yarn:
Choose a thin, less stretchy yarn for this project, so it won't be too heavy to wear around your neck.

 Tension:
For this project, try to knit loosely, without pulling the stitches too tight. This will make the knitted fabric lighter and more supple.

Pink hat

This hat is made from the top down, with the shaping coming from increasing. You can also shape a hat from the bottom up, by decreasing stitches (see the blue beanie on page 24).

- 12 mm crochet hook
- 1 ball of pink T-shirt yarn
- scissors
- yarn needle

Start with a ring: Chain 5, then slip stitch in the first chain to form a ring.

Single crochet in each stitch around. After the first round, increase gradually by working 2 stitches in some stitches. How often you increase will depend on the thickness and elasticity of the particular T-shirt yarn you are using, as well as on how tightly or loosely you crochet. For a perfect fit, try the hat on frequently to check its shape. If the hat bulges, you have increased too quickly; unravel the last few rounds and try again, spacing the increases out more. If the hat is too tight, you need to increase more.

Stop increasing when the hat is as big around as your head. Crochet one round even, without increasing or decreasing.

Adjust the fit of your hat by decreasing gradually over the next few rows. Don't hesitate to try the hat on in the middle of a row to test the fit. Continue until the bottom edge of the hat reaches your ears.

Work one row of slip stitches around the bottom of the hat, working through both loops of each stitch, then work a second row of slip stitches, working through the back loop only of each stitch of the previous row.

Fasten off and use a yarn needle to weave the yarn ends into the fabric.

 Tip:

When working in the round, it can be hard to keep track of where each round begins and ends. To help yourself remember, you can mark the first stitch of each round by threading a piece of scrap yarn in a different color through it.

 The flower:

Make three loops of T-shirt yarn, then tie them together at the base. Tie the flower formed to the beanie with the knot on the inside.

 Your choice:

This hat pattern is reversible: You choose which side of the fabric you prefer.

Leg warmers

These quick and easy leg warmers will keep your ankles warm when dancing or going out on a chilly day.

- a pair of 12 mm straight knitting needles
- 1 ball of light pink T-shirt yarn
- scissors
- yarn needle

Cast on 25 stitches onto one needle.

Mark the other needle by tying a piece of colored yarn to the end. This will help you keep track of when to work purl stitches.

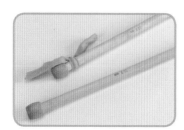

Work in stockinette stitch as follows: Knit the first row, then purl the next row. Continue to alternate between knit and purl rows.

Stop when the piece measures 11 in. (28 cm)—about 28 rows, but the exact number will depend on the thickness of your yarn and how tightly you knit.

Bind off the stitches and fasten off, leaving a long tail to use when assembling the project.

Fold the piece with the right side in and bring the cast-on and bind-off edges together to create a tube.

Use the long tail and a yarn needle to sew the edges together.

Repeat from step 1 to make a second leg warmer.

 Tip:
Choose a thin T-shirt yarn for this project so the leg warmers won't be too heavy.

 Keeping track:
Remember to purl when working stitches from the marked needle to the unmarked needle and knit when working in the opposite direction.

 Reversible:
If you sew the seam neatly, these leg warmers are completely reversible.

Fuchsia laptop bag

The combination of handles and strap makes this laptop bag very practical to use.

- 12 mm crochet hook
- 1 ball of fuchsia T-shirt yarn
- 1 premade strap
- scissors
- yarn needle

 1

Start with the two narrow ends: Chain 26. Slip stitch in the second chain from the hook and in each stitch to the end of the chain, working in the back loop only of each stitch.

 2

Work 3 slip stitches in the last chain to go around the end.

 3

Work slip stitches up the other side of the chain back to the beginning, working in the unworked loops of the stitches. When you get to the first stitch, work 2 stitches in it. Go around the whole piece 5 more times, working a slip stitch in the back loop of every stitch. Finish with a slip stitch in the end of the piece, then fasten off the work. Use a yarn needle to weave the yarn end into the fabric.

 4

Repeat steps 1 through 3 to make another narrow end.

 5

Next, make the large rectangle that will form the body of the bag. Start by chaining 26.

 6

Single crochet in the second chain from the hook and in each chain across, working through both loops of each stitch. At the end of the row, chain 1 and then turn the work. Continue to work back and forth in single crochet until the piece is long enough to go all the way around the narrow ends.

 7

Attach the main body of the bag to the narrow ends by working single crochet through both pieces of fabric around each end.

 8

Add the handles: Join the yarn at one end of the top opening of the bag. Working across one long side, single crochet in the first 5 stitches, working through both loops of each stitch. Chain 15 and skip the next 15 stitches, then single crochet in the last 5 stitches of the edge.

 9

Chain 1, then turn the work and work back along the side, working 1 single crochet in each stitch or chain. Fasten off. Repeat steps 8 and 9 on the other side of the purse to add the other handle.

 Tip:
Choose a thick T-shirt yarn for this project so your bag will be sturdy enough to hold a heavy laptop.

 Three pieces:
This bag is constructed in three pieces: Two small side pieces and a large rectangle that wraps around them to form the front, back, and bottom of the bag. This rectangle is attached to the edges of the small pieces.

 The straps:
Use a yarn needle or your crochet hook to attach the rings for the strap to the tops of the short ends of the bag.

Beige beret

This beret is made from a combination of slip stitches and single crochets. Once it is finished, you can choose which side of the fabric you prefer to wear on the outside.

- 12 mm crochet hook
- 1 ball of beige T-shirt yarn
- scissors
- yarn needle

Chain 5. Slip stitch in the first chain to join into a ring.

Slip stitch in each chain around the ring, working in the back loop only of each stitch.

After the first round, increase in every other stitch by working 2 stitches in the same stitch.

Continue to work in a spiral around, increasing to keep the piece as flat as possible, until the piece measures about 12 in. (30 cm) in diameter.

Begin to decrease, skipping every 6th stitch on the first decrease round. On the next round skip every 4th stitch, and on the third decrease round skip every 3rd stitch.

Try the hat on frequently to check the fit, and adjust how much and how quickly you decrease stitches in order to get the fit you want.

When the hat is as large around as your head, stop decreasing and work two rounds even in single crochet, working through both loops of each stitch.

End the last round with a slip stitch in the first stitch of the round. Fasten off.

Use a yarn needle to weave the yarn ends into the fabric to hide them.

 Tip:
Choose a thin T-shirt yarn for this project for a lightweight beanie that is easy to wear.

 It's bulging!
If your fabric warps or bulges, you are increasing too quickly. Unravel the last few rows and increase more gradually.

 The walls are closing in . . .
If the circle in steps 3 and 4 closes in on itself like a bowl, you haven't increased enough. Pull out the last few rows and try again, increasing more frequently.

Millefiori purse

The charm of this purse is in its simple design, which shows off the pretty flecked yarn it was made with. You can also try multicolored yarns in this design. The small size is perfect for carrying a paperback, a tablet, or a small bunch of flowers.

- 12 mm crochet hook
- 1 ball of patterned or multicolored T-shirt yarn
- scissors
- yarn needle
- tape measure
- 1 premade handle

1 Determine how far apart you want the ends of the handle to be.

2 Start with a slip knot on your crochet hook and work as many chains as you need to reach from one end of the handle to the other end with the two ends the desired distance apart.

3 Count the chain stitches, then add one more for a turning chain.

4 Single crochet in the second chain from the hook and in each chain along the starting chain, working through the back loop only of each chain.

5 When you get to the last chain, work 3 stitches in it to turn and continue along the other side of the chain, working through the unworked loops.

6 When you get to the end of the chain, work 3 stitches in the last stitch.

7 Continue to work around the piece in single crochet, working through the back loop only of each stitch. Bit by bit, the purse will grow and take its shape.

8 When the purse is 8 in. (20 cm) deep, stop. Work a slip stitch in the next stitch, then fasten off the work.

9 Using the same yarn you used to make the purse and a yarn needle, sew each end of the handle to one end of the top opening of the purse. Use the yarn needle to weave any yarn ends into the fabric.

 Tip:
Choose your handle before starting to make the purse, as the size of the handle will determine the size of the purse.

 Closure:
If you want to close the top of this purse, you can add a loop and a little button like the ones shown on the tube purse on page 26.

 Idea:
Instead of using a yarn needle to sew the ends of the handle to the purse, you could crochet through them a few times.

54

42

46

60

62

50

56

52

Home Décor

44

Two-color catchall

This fabric basket is quick to make and doesn't require a lot of yarn. The leftovers from a skein used for another project will work quite well.

- 12 mm crochet hook
- small amount of blue T-shirt yarn
- small amount of white T-shirt yarn
- scissors
- yarn needle

With blue, chain 12. Single crochet in the second chain from the hook and in each chain across, working through the back loop only of each stitch.

Chain 1, turn the work, and single crochet in each stitch across, still working in the back loop only of each stitch. Continue to work back and forth in this manner until you have completed 10 rows.

In the last stitch of the tenth row, change to the white yarn by working the stitch up to the last yarn over, then completing the stitch (yarn over, pull through both loops on hook) with the white yarn. Cut the blue yarn, leaving a short tail.

Chain 1, turn, and single crochet in each stitch across through the back loop only. Work 44 rows in all with the white yarn.

Change back to the blue yarn in the same way as before, in the last stitch of the last white row.

Cut the white yarn and continue in blue for 10 more rows. Fasten off.

Fold the beginning blue section over onto the white part to form a pocket.

Sew the pocket in place by working slip stitch along the edge, working through both layers of fabric from the back of the work.

Repeat steps 7 and 8 with the other pocket. Use a yarn needle to weave the yarn ends into the fabric.

Adapting the pattern:
As always, the number of stitches and rows given in the instructions is a suggestion only. Feel free to add or omit stitches or rows to adapt the project to your needs.

Tip:
Choose a thick yarn for this project to make your catchall sturdy.

Assembly:
If you prefer, you can sew the pockets to the backing with a yarn needle and the blue T-shirt yarn instead of crocheting them.

Green basket

This pattern is particularly customizable to whatever size and shape you want. Because every recycled yarn has a different thickness and elasticity, you may find that you need to adjust the rate of increasing for shaped projects like this one. The upside to using T-shirt yarn is that you can do and undo stitches over and over and the yarn will not unravel.

- 12 mm crochet hook
- 1 ball of green T-shirt yarn
- scissors
- yarn needle

1

Chain 5. Slip stitch in the first chain to form a ring.

2

Single crochet in each stitch around the ring, working through the back loop only of each stitch.

3

Single crochet in the first stitch of the round to continue around the piece in a spiral.

4

Increase in every other stitch by working 2 stitches into 1 stitch, still working through the back loop only of each stitch.

5

Continue around, increasing steadily to keep the work flat, until your piece is the desired size for the bottom of your basket.

6

Work several rounds even, without increasing or decreasing, to make the sides of the basket. Continue until you have reached just under the desired depth for the basket.

7

Work one more row, decreasing a few stitches evenly around the row to draw in the top of the basket.

8

Slip stitch in the next stitch to even out the end of the round, then fasten off. Use a yarn needle to weave the yarn ends into the fabric.

 Tip:

Choose a thick, stretchy yarn for this project, which will give you a basket with sturdy, even walls.

 Not flat enough:

If the bottom of your basket is not flat enough, you need to increase more often: Try increasing in 2 stitches out of every 3. (Increase in two stitches in a row and work the third normally, then repeat.)

 Too floppy:

If the edge of the piece buckles or bulges, you are increasing too often. Try increasing in every third stitch.

Toy box

This big, soft toy box is a great place to keep your little one's favorite stuffed toys—when they're not being carried along on adventures.

- 12 mm crochet hook
- 3 balls of beige T-shirt yarn
- 1 ball of navy blue T-shirt yarn
- scissors
- yarn needle

1

Chain 41.

2

Single crochet in the second chain from the hook and in each chain across, working through the back loop only of each stitch.

3

Chain 1, turn the work, and single crochet across, still working through the back loops only. Continue to work back and forth for 30 rows. Fasten off.

4

Repeat steps 1–3 to make a second long rectangle.

5

For the short sides, chain 21, then work back and forth in single crochet through the back loops only for 30 rows. Make 2 short sides.

6

Make the bottom: Chain 41, then work back and forth in single crochet through the back loops only for about 20 rows, or until the piece is as wide as the base of the short sides.

7

Place the four sides around the bottom piece. Use single crochet to attach the pieces together along the edges.

8

Join the navy blue yarn by placing a slip knot on the crochet hook and then working a slip stitch through any stitch along the top edge. Work a row of single crochet all the way around the top edge, working through both loops of each stitch. Work a second row of single crochet in the same way.

9

On the third border row, skip every 4th stitch (see page 10). This will draw in the opening a bit and give the box extra stability. Use a yarn needle to weave the yarn ends into the fabric.

 Seams:

When assembling the box, place the pieces with the right sides together while you sew the seams if you want to hide the seams (as shown in the toy box pictured). If you want the seams to be visible, work with the wrong sides of the pieces together.

 Tip:

For a firmer, sturdier bottom of the box, you can make two bottom pieces and sew them together with a piece of cardboard in between before attaching the sides to the box.

 Variation:

If you make a smaller version of this box, you might want to add handles like the ones used in the laptop bag on page 34 to make the toy box easier to carry around.

Tricolored ottoman cover

Dress up an old, worn-out ottoman in new colors to give it new life! You can make this footstool cover in jewel tones, as shown here, or match the colors to your décor.

- a pair of 12 mm straight knitting needles
- 2 balls of pink T-shirt yarn
- 1 ball of purple T-shirt yarn
- 2 balls of fuchsia T-shirt yarn
- scissors
- measuring tape
- yarn needle

 Measure the ottoman you want to cover.

 Cast on enough stitches to reach the required length for a side. Our T-shirt yarn gave about 5 stitches for every 2 in. (5 cm), but depending on the particular yarn you use, the size of your needles, and how tightly you knit, you might have different results. To be sure, knit a small test square to see how many stitches you get to the inch.

 Work in garter stitch—knit every row—until the piece is as tall as you need it to be.

 Count your rows, either while you knit or after you finish the square, so you can make the other sides the same size.

 When the side is the required height, bind off the stitches and fasten off the work.

 Repeat steps 2–5 to make the other 3 sides. If your ottoman is not square, adjust the size of two of the sides accordingly.

 Finally, make the panel for the top of the ottoman, still in garter stitch. Ours is the same size as the sides, but if your ottoman is a different shape, this piece may be different from the sides.

 Assemble the pieces into a cube with no bottom, either by single crocheting or slip stitching the sides together or by sewing them together with a yarn needle (see page 11); use whichever technique you prefer.

 Use a yarn needle to weave the yarn ends into the fabric. Turn the project inside out (unless you prefer the seams to be visible).

 Tip:
Choose three yarns that are similar in thickness and elasticity for this project; this will make the finished piece more consistent.

 Construction:
This project is composed of 5 pieces: 4 side panels and 1 top panel.

 Design:
Assemble your ottoman cover with the sides in pairs—the two pink sides touching on one edge and the two fuchsia sides touching on an edge. This way, the ottoman cover will appear three-colored from one angle and two-colored from another.

Neon pillow covers

One, two, three pillows in flourescent colors.
Brighten up your living room with a bit of crochet!

- 12 mm crochet hook
- 1 ball of patterned pink T-shirt yarn
- 1 ball of magenta T-shirt yarn
- 1 ball of lime green T-shirt yarn
- tape measure
- scissors
- yarn needle

Choose a pillow to cover and measure one side. (If the pillow is a rectangle, this can be either a long side or a short side. Of the pillow covers shown in the photo, the pink ones were made based on the short side of the pillow and the green one was made based on the long side.)

Make a chain as long as the side length. Our T-shirt yarn gave about 5 stitches for every 2 in. (5 cm), but depending on the particular yarn you use, the size of your crochet hook, and how tightly you crochet, you might have different results. To be sure, crochet a small test square to see how many stitches you get to the inch.

Single crochet in the second chain from the hook and in each chain across. You can work through the back loop only if you want ridges on the fabric (as in the pink pillows pictured); if you want a smoother fabric (like the green pillow), work through both loops of every stitch. (See page 11 for more information about different ways of working into a stitch.)

Chain 1, turn the work, and single crochet as in step 3 to the other end.

Continue to work back and forth in rows until the piece is long enough to cover one side of the pillow. Fasten off.

Repeat steps 2–5 to make a rectangle for the back of the pillow.

Place the two rectangles together and slip stitch around the edges through both layers of fabric to assemble them (see page 11). Slip the pillow inside the cover before closing the last side. Fasten off and use a yarn needle to weave the yarn ends into the fabric.

 Note:

If you start the pillow based on a short side, the ridges formed by the rows will be vertical (if the long side of the pillow is the horizontal); if you start along a long side, the rows will run horizontally.

 Don't forget:

Remember to always chain 1 at the end of every row before turning the work, so that you keep a constant number of stitches in each row.

 Contrast:

You can choose any color to work the seams of this pillow—either the same color you used for the body of the pillow for a uniform look, or a different color for contrast.

Beige footstool

This round slipcover is built in a spiral, like a snail shell. It's perfect for giving new life to a worn-out ottoman.

- 12 mm crochet hook
- 2 balls of beige yarn
- scissors
- yarn needle

 1

Chain 5. Slip stitch in the first chain to form a ring.

 2

Single crochet in each stitch around the ring, working through the back loop only of each stitch.

 3

When you get to the end of the round, single crochet in the first stitch in the round to continue around in a continuous spiral. Continue around, increasing in every other stitch and still working through the back loop only, for 4 rounds.

 4

Work around, reducing how often you increase as necessary to keep the work flat; exactly how often will depend on how stretchy your yarn is and how tightly you crochet.

 5

When your piece is the size of the top of your ottoman, stop increasing.

 6

Work around evenly, without increasing or decreasing, to form the sides. Try the cover on over your ottoman often to check the fit.

 7

When the cover is long enough to cover the sides of your ottoman, begin decreasing. Skip every 10th stitch in the first round, then skip every 8th stitch in the second round. In the final decrease round, skip every 5th stitch.

 8

As always, you can adjust the number of rows or the shaping to better fit your needs. When you are happy with the fit of the cover, fasten off the work and use a yarn needle to weave the yarn ends into the fabric.

 Increasing:

Pay attention to the piece: If it bulges, you need to reduce the frequency of increases.

 Decreasing:

Don't decrease too often, or the piece will close too abruptly and not fit correctly.

 The bottom:

Don't close the bottom of the case entirely, or you won't be able to put it on the ottoman (or take it off to clean it).

Multicolor basket

This multicolored basket is a lovely decorative container.
The little handles allow you to carry it anywhere you want.

- 12 mm crochet hook
- 1 ball of multicolored
  T-shirt yarn
- scissors
- yarn needle

1
Chain 5. Slip stitch in the first chain to form a ring.

2
Work 2 single crochets in the first stitch of the ring, working through the back loop only of the stitch. Work 1 single crochet through the back loop of the next stitch.

3
Continue around in this same pattern: 2 stitches in one stitch, then 1 stitch in the next.

4
Stop increasing when the piece measures 8 in. (20 cm) in diameter.

5
Form the sides by continuing around evenly, without increasing or decreasing, still working through the back loop only of each stitch.

6
Work 10 rounds even.

7
Make the handles by chaining 10, then skipping the next 8 stitches of the basket and continuing to single crochet in the next stitch. Single crochet around to the opposite side of the basket and chain 10 and skip another 8 stitches to create the second handle opposite the first.

8
Work another full row of single crochet in each stitch and chain around the top edge, then slip stitch in the first stitch of the row to even out the end of the row, then fasten off. Use a yarn needle to weave the yarn ends into the fabric.

 The bottom:
The circle that forms the bottom of the basket needs to be flat. If the bottom bulges, pull out a few rows and try again, increasing in every 3rd stitch instead of every other stitch.

 Working in the round:
It can be easy to lose track of where the rounds begin and end when working in continuous rounds. To help keep track, thread a piece of scrap yarn in a contrasting color through the first stitch of every round. Take the piece of yarn out when you finish the round and move it up to the first stitch of the new round.

 Your choice:
This basket is reversible: It's up to you to choose which side of the fabric you prefer for the outside.

Round blue rug

A bathroom rug made from soft, fluffy cotton yarn . . .
could there be a nicer way to get out of the shower?

- 12 mm crochet hook
- 2 balls of gray-blue T-shirt yarn
- scissors
- yarn needle

 1

Chain 5. Slip stitch in the first chain to form a ring.

 2

Work 2 single crochet stitches in the next chain, working through the back loop only.

 3

Work 1 single crochet in the next chain.

 4

Continue in this pattern, working 2 stitches in one stitch and 1 stitch in the next stitch. When you get to the end of the round, continue the pattern by working 1 stitch into the first stitch of the round; continue around in a continous spiral, like a snail shell.

 5

As the rug grows, lay it out flat frequently to check the shape. If the piece curls up around the edges like a bowl, you need to increase more often—try increasing 2 times over every 3 stitches. If the piece bulges or ripples around the edges, you are increasing too quickly. In this case, try increasing only every 3 stitches. It's completely possible that you might have to increase and decrease in the same round. Observe the way the piece is growing and adapt your stitches to suit the idiosyncracies of your yarn.

 6

Stop when your rug measures about 30 in. (80 cm) in diameter. Finish by working a slip stitch in the next stitch to even out the end of the round.

 7

Fasten off the work and use a yarn needle to weave the yarn ends into the fabric.

 The stitches:

This rug is worked entirely in single crochet worked through the back loop only of each stitch.

 Tip:

To better control the shape of your rug, work on or near a table so you can lay it out flat frequently. This will allow you to see if you need to add or omit stitches.

 Variation:

If you have lots of small amounts of yarn left over from other projects, use them for a striped hit-or-miss rug. Have fun with the combinations of colors.

Bathroom baskets

Customize these little baskets to your needs; pick the size, color, and lid style you like best.

- 12 mm crochet hook
- 1 ball of pink T-shirt yarn
- 1 ball of teal T-shirt yarn
- 1 ball of multicolored T-shirt yarn
- tape measure
- scissors
- yarn needle

 1

Chain 5, then work a slip stitch in the first chain to form a ring (see page 10).

 2

Single crochet in the first stitch of the ring, working through the back loop only.

 3

Continue crocheting around the ring, increasing in every other stitch, to form a circle for the bottom of the basket. Adjust the frequency of increases as needed to keep the piece flat: If it pulls in like a bowl, increase more often (2 times over every 3 stitches); if it bulges or ripples on the edges, increase less often (1 time every 3 stitches). Continue around until the piece is the desired size. The baskets shown here are 3, 5, and 6 in. (8, 13, and 15 cm) in diameter.

 4

Work 1 single crochet in each stitch for the next round. If you want a defined edge between the base and the sides (like in the multicolored basket in the photo), work through the front loop only. If you want a more rounded edge to the bottom of your basket (like the other two baskets), work through the back loop only.

 5

Continue to work around evenly, without increasing or decreasing, working through the back loops only (even if you chose to work through the front loop for the first round of the sides).

 6

Crochet around the sides for 6 to 10 rounds, or until the basket reaches the desired height. Finish by working a slip stitch in the next stitch to even out the end of the round. Fasten off.

 7

To make the lid, start from step 1 again.

 8

Stop at the end of step 3 for a flat lid, or continue through step 4 for a lid with a lip, like the one on the green basket in the photo. Work a slip stitch in the next stitch to even out the end of the round, then fasten off. Use a yarn needle to weave the yarn ends into the fabric on both the basket and the lid. Use the end from the beginning of the lid to form a loop, if desired.

 Customizing the project:

You have a lot of choices in this project. The lid can be flat or lipped. The basket can be turned to have either side of the fabric on the outside. The base can be rounded with a defined edge. Each basket in the photo shows a different combination of options.

 The bottom of the basket:

The way you work the first round of the sides determines how the edges of the base will be: Working through the back loop = a rounded edge; working through the front loop = a sharp edge.

 The loop:

The little loop on the top of the lid is made from the yarn tail from the beginning of the lid. Decide which side of the lid will be the right side, then hide the knot on the other side.

Coffee and cream pillows

These pillow covers are knitted with different stitches and yarns with different textures. If you prefer crochet to knitting, take a look at the neon pillow covers on page 50.

- a pair of 12 mm straight knitting needles
- 1 ball of off-white T-shirt yarn
- 1 ball of beige T-shirt yarn
- 1 ball of light brown T-shirt yarn
- scissors
- yarn needle

Measure one side of the pillow you want to cover and cast on enough stitches to cover that length. Our T-shirt yarn gave about 5 stitches for every 2 in. (5 cm), but depending on the particular yarn you use, the size of your needles, and how tightly you knit, you might have different results. To be sure, knit a small test square to see how many stitches you get to the inch.

For a garter stitch pillow (the white and brown pillows in the photo), knit every row (see page 6).

For a stockinette stitch pillow (the beige pillow in the photo), alternate rows of knit stitches and purl stitches.

Work back and forth until the piece is long enough to cover a full side of the pillow. Bind off the stitches and fasten off.

Make a second panel the same as the first one: one for the front of the pillow, the other for the back.

If you want the seam to be hidden, as in the white and beige pillows in the photo, place the pieces with right sides together. If you want the seam to be visible, as in the brown pillow, place the pieces with wrong sides together.

Assemble the pieces on 3 sides, either by sewing them together or by working single crochet along the edge, working through both pieces of fabric.

Turn the piece right side out (if you are doing a variation with hidden seams) and slide the pillow inside before sewing the last side closed.

 Note:
The firmness of the pillow will depend on the elasticity and thickness of your yarn, as well as how tightly you knit. The brown pillow in the photo is very soft and supple, while the beige pillow is much tighter and firmer.

 The stitch count:
The number of stitches will vary depending on the size of your pillow—but also on the particular yarn you use. A starting rule of thumb is 1 stitch = ½ in. (1 cm), but check the width of your piece before you knit the whole thing.

 Edging:
It's up to you whether you want to assemble your pillow with matching yarn or with a contrasting color for a border, as in the brown pillow.

Coral-pink baby blanket

This little blanket will protect baby from drafts during a promenade in a stroller or an afternoon nap in a bassinet.

- a pair of 12 mm straight knitting needles
- 2 balls of coral T-shirt yarn
- 1 ball of magenta T-shirt yarn
- scissors
- yarn needle

Cast on 20 stitches onto one knitting needle with the main yarn color.

Mark the other needle by tying a short length of yarn in another color to the end.

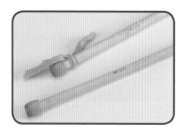

Work 60 rows in stockinette stitch—that is, alternating between rows of knit stitches and purl stitches. Use the marked needle to keep track of which row you're on: When you're working stitches from the unmarked needle onto the marked needle, knit every stitch. When working stitches in the other direction, from the marked needle onto the unmarked needle, purl the stitches.

After 60 rows, bind off the stitches, cut the yarn, and use the yarn needle to weave the yarn ends into the fabric.

Repeat steps 1–4 to knit a second strip just like the first.

Now knit a third strip for the middle of the blanket. Cast on 20 stitches and work in stockinette stitch in the main color for 20 rows. After 20 rows, change to the contrasting color by simply working each stitch with the new color and cutting the old yarn, leaving a tail to weave in later. (There is no need to bind off stitches when changing colors.)

Work in garter stitch—knit every row—with the contrasting color for 20 rows.

Switch back to the main color and knit 20 more rows in stockinette stitch. Bind off the stitches and use a yarn needle to weave in all the ends on this strip.

Use a yarn needle to sew the 3 strips together with the one with the garter stitch section in the middle. Weave any ends from the sewing yarn into the fabric to hide them.

 Counting rows:

To help keep track of where you are in the number of rows, remember that the stitches will always end up on the marked needle at the end of every odd-numbered row.

 Variations:

This blanket is made mostly in stockinette stitch, but you could also make it in seed stitch (see page 28) or all in garter stitch (see page 48).

 Finishing:

If the edges of the blanket curl up on themselves, thread a length of yarn through the stitches of each edge using a yarn needle to stabilize the edges. You can also work a border of single crochet around the edge of the blanket, working 3 stitches in each corner so they lie flat.